Friendship Shawl.org

The intriguing words above are the first thing you'll see when you visit the Web site of the Friendship Shawl organization. You'll learn more about this group of caring knitters and crocheters as you read best-selling author Debbie Macomber's welcome letter. Debbie explains the heartwarming charity idea of creating shawls for loved ones and those in need. While you visit the site of this Warm Up America! initiative, you'll find free stitch patterns you can use to make shawls, a listing of color meanings to help you choose yarn, and a page where knitters and crocheters tell their inspiring friendship shawl stories.

FriendshipShawl.org

Warm Up America.org

...wrapping people in warm blankets since 1992

Warm Up America! is a nationwide foundation that coordinates the efforts of volunteers who knit and crochet afghans to help those in need. Through their efforts, thousands of afghans are sent each year to hospitals, nursing homes, shelters, American Red Cross chapters, and other social service agencies. Debbie urges everyone who knits to make a 7" x 9" block for this worthy cause. On page 4 of this book, she is providing a pattern for a knitted block to get you started. Please donate completed afghans to a charity or social services agency in your area. If you are unable to assemble your blocks, include your name and address inside the packaging and ship your blocks to:

Warm Up America! Foundation
2500 Lowell Road
Ranlo, North Carolina 28054

Remember, just a little bit of yarn can make a big difference to someone in need!

Diamonds block

Multiple of 10 sts + 1.

Cast on 31 sts.

Row 1 (Right side)**:** K5, P1, K3, P1, K1, P1, ★ (K3, P1) twice, K1, P1; repeat from ★ across to last 9 sts, K3, P1, K5.

Row 2: P5, K1, P3, K1, P1, K1, ★ (P3, K1) twice, P1, K1; repeat from ★ across to last 9 sts, P3, K1, P5.

Row 3: K4, P1, K1, P1, ★ (K3, P1) twice, K1, P1; repeat from ★ across to last 4 sts, K4.

Row 4: P4, K1, P1, K1, ★ (P3, K1) twice, P1, K1; repeat from ★ across to last 4 sts, P4.

Row 5: K3, P1, (K1, P1) twice, ★ (K2, P1) twice, (K1, P1) twice; repeat from ★ across to last 3 sts, K3.

Row 6: P3, K1, (P1, K1) twice, ★ (P2, K1) twice, (P1, K1) twice; repeat from ★ across to last 3 sts, P3.

Row 7: K4, P1, K1, P1, ★ (K3, P1) twice, K1, P1; repeat from ★ across to last 4 sts, K4.

Row 8: P4, K1, P1, K1, ★ (P3, K1) twice, P1, K1; repeat from ★ across to last 4 sts, P4.

Row 9: K5, P1, K3, P1, K1, P1, ★ (K3, P1) twice, K1, P1; repeat from ★ across to last 9 sts, K3, P1, K5.

Row 10: P5, K1, P3, K1, P1, K1, ★ (P3, K1) twice, P1, K1; repeat from ★ across to last 9 sts, P3, K1, P5.

Row 11: K5, P1, K2, P1, (K1, P1) twice, ★ (K2, P1) twice, (K1, P1) twice; repeat from ★ across to last 8 sts, K2, P1, K5.

Row 12: P5, K1, P2, K1, (P1, K1) twice, ★ (P2, K1) twice, (P1, K1) twice; repeat from ★ across to last 8 sts, P2, K1, P5.

Repeat Rows 1-12 for pattern until Block measures approximately 9" (23 cm) from cast on edge, ending by working a **wrong** side row.

Bind off all sts in **knit**.

a letter from Debbie macomber

With more than 100 million copies of her books in print, Debbie Macomber's compelling stories touch hearts all over the world.

As her readers know, Debbie is an avid knitter who enjoys drawing attention to her favorite children's charities: Warm Up America!, Project Linus, Guideposts Knit for Kids, and World Vision. In fact, Debbie donates all her proceeds from sales of her Leisure Arts *Knit Along* books and her new Knit Along with Debbie Macomber product line (see page 2) to these charities.

The best-selling author lives in the Northwest with husband Wayne. Debbie enjoys the company of her four children and eight grandchildren whenever possible.

Dear Friends,

When knitting gives me a new way to encourage others, I can't help but get excited about it. That's why I'm so pleased that Leisure Arts asked me to be a part of publishing this book of friendship shawl patterns.

Similar to prayer shawls, friendship shawls are knitted or crocheted as gifts of caring. They're perfect for special occasions such as birthdays or anniversaries, and make wonderful "just because" gifts for dear friends. And the giving can go beyond helping the folks you know—people in shelters, nursing homes, and hospitals also need your handmade shawls.

If you're ready to get started, the **ten knit friendship shawls** in this book will inspire your creativity. Just imagine making that gorgeous red wrap on page 7 for your best friend, or the soft blue Thinking of You Shawl on page 19 for someone who's under the weather!

My friends at Warm Up America! invite you to visit **FriendshipShawl.org** and read the stories of individuals whose lives have been enriched by knitted and crocheted wraps—maybe I'll see your story there soon. While you're online, I would love it if you would stop by **DebbieMacomber.com** to read my blog and see what's new in my corner of the world. I look forward to hearing from you!

Debbie

LEISURE ARTS, INC.
Little Rock, Arkansas

a word from
LEISURE ARTS
and MIRA books

Three Exciting Ways to knit along with
DEBBIE MACOMBER

Knitting friend, be sure to visit MiraBooks.com regularly so you don't miss a single Debbie Macomber book! The characters in Debbie's tales of love and friendship are often knitters, just like you!

For more knitting fun, click on over to TheLeisureBoutique.com to find all the *Knit Along With Debbie Macomber* pattern books from Leisure Arts. Many of the patterns are based on projects created by characters in Debbie's books.

And here's the newest way you can knit with Debbie: All of these wonderful publications inspired a stylish collection of accessories for today's knitters! The Knit Along With Debbie Macomber Collection includes an ingenious journal/CD set, beautiful totes and storage options, a purse kit, classic patterns, and handy knitting notions. You can see the complete line at TheLeisureBoutique.com or at your favorite knitting shop.

READ DEBBIE MACOMBER'S HEARTWARMING STORIES.

COLLECT THE *KNIT ALONG WITH DEBBIE MACOMBER* PATTERN BOOKS.

AND NOW, PAMPER YOURSELF WITH DEBBIE'S NEW LINE OF KNITTING ACCESSORIES!

Leaflet# 4279

To find out more about Debbie Macomber, visit **debbiemacomber.com** or **mirabooks.com.**

the art of everyday living

For more information about these and other Leisure Arts publications, call 1.800.526.5111 or visit **www.TheLeisureBoutique.com.**

The Meanings of colors

Whether you create a friendship shawl for a celebration or just to show you care, you may find a color that symbolizes the sentiment you want your shawl to convey. Listed below are traditional meanings for several colors. At **FriendshipShawl.org**, you can also find a listing of some of the colors used to represent well-known charities and causes.

COLOR MEANINGS

Red	Energy, strength, power, determination, love, courage
Pink	Joy, friendship, femininity
Brown	Stability, masculinity
Orange	Happiness, success, encouragement, endurance
Gold	Illumination, wisdom
Yellow	Cheerfulness, energy, joy, confidence
Green	Healing, harmony, safety, hope, protection, peace
Blue	Stability, trust, loyalty, faith, truth, tranquility
Purple	Wisdom, dignity, independence, creativity, mystery
White	Goodness, purity, innocence, faith, safety, light

BIRTHSTONE COLORS

Another fun method for choosing yarn color is to base your selection on the recipient's birthstone color.

MONTH	GEM	GEM COLOR
January	Garnet	dark red
February	Amethyst	purple
March	Aquamarine	pale blue
April	Diamond	clear
May	Emerald	green
June	Pearl	cream
July	Ruby	bright red
August	Peridot	pale green
September	Sapphire	dark blue
October	Opal	variegated
November	Topaz	yellow
December	Turquoise	sky blue

for All reasons

🔴⬜⬜⬜ **BEGINNER**

Finished Size: 20¹/₂" x 72" (52 cm x 183 cm)

MATERIALS
Bulky Weight Yarn **5** BULKY
[3.52 ounces, 124 yards
(100 grams, 114 meters) per skein]:
5 skeins
Straight knitting needles, size 10¹/₂ (6.5 mm)
or size needed for gauge

GAUGE: In pattern, 10 sts = 3³/₄" (9.5 cm)

Gauge Swatch: 3³/₄"w (9.5 cm)
Cast on 10 sts.
Row 1: K5, P5.
Row 2: Purl across.
Repeat Rows 1 and 2 for 4" (10 cm).
Bind off all sts in **purl**.

> Each row is worked across the width of the Shawl and can be worked to any length.

SHAWL
Cast on 55 sts.

Rows 1-8: Purl across.

Row 9 (Right side)**:** P5, (K5, P5) across.

Row 10: Purl across.

Repeat Rows 9 and 10 for pattern until Shawl measures approximately 70¹/₂" (179 cm) from cast on edge, ending by working Row 9.

Last 8 Rows: Purl across.

Bind off all sts in **purl**.

Design by Cathy Hardy.

A Hug to keep

Finished Size: 70¹/₂" wide x 36" deep
(179 cm x 91.5 cm)

MATERIALS

Bulky Weight Brushed Acrylic or Mohair Blend Yarn
[1.75 ounces, 89 yards
(50 grams, 82 meters) per skein]:
6 skeins
29" (73.5 cm) Circular knitting needle,
size 10¹/₂ (6.5 mm) **or** size needed for gauge

GAUGE: In Stockinette Stitch,
12 sts and 18 rows = 4" (10 cm)

> This Shawl begins at the bottom tip and is worked up. Shaping is achieved by adding on stitches using the knit cast on method *(Figs. 5a-e, pages 42 & 43)* in a stair-step fashion.

SHAWL

Cast on 4 sts.

Rows 1-6: Knit across.

Rows 7 and 8: Add on 4 sts; knit across: 12 sts.

Rows 9-12: Knit across.

Row 13 (Right side)**:** Add on 4 sts; knit across: 16 sts.

Row 14: Add on 4 sts; K8, P4, K8: 20 sts.

Row 15: Knit across.

Row 16: K8, P4, K8.

Rows 17 and 18: Repeat Rows 15 and 16.

Row 19: Add on 4 sts; knit across: 24 sts.

Row 20: Add on 4 sts; K8, purl across to last 8 sts, K8: 28 sts.

Row 21: Knit across.

Row 22: K8, purl across to last 8 sts, K8.

Rows 23 and 24: Repeat Rows 21 and 22.

Repeat Rows 19-24 for pattern until Shawl measures approximately 35" (89 cm) from cast on edge **or** 1" (2.5 cm) less than desired length, ending by working Row 24.

Last 6 Rows: Repeat Rows 7-12.

Bind off all sts in **knit**.

Design by Cathy Hardy.

Because I care

Finished Size: 72" wide x 36" deep
(183 cm x 91.5 cm)

MATERIALS
Bulky Weight Yarn
[3.5 ounces, 121 yards
(100 grams, 110 meters) per skein]:
   7 skeins
29" (73.5 cm) Circular knitting needle,
   size 10 (6 mm) **or** size needed for gauge
Markers

GAUGE: In pattern,
   14 sts and 20 rows = 4" (10 cm)

Gauge Swatch: 4" (10 cm) square
Cast on 14 sts.
Row 1: Knit across.
Row 2: (K1, P1) across.
Rows 3-20: Repeat Rows 1 and 2, 9 times.
Bind off all sts in **knit**.

This Shawl begins at the center of the neck and is worked down. The end of rows form the neck edge and the YO increases form the triangular shape. Knit stitches will form vertical lines with Garter Stitch in between.

SHAWL
Cast on 3 sts.

Row 1 (Right side): K1, (YO, K1) twice (**Fig. 8a, page 44**): 5 sts.

Row 2: P1, (K1, P1) twice.

Row 3: (K1, YO) twice, place marker (**see Markers, page 41**), K1, (YO, K1) twice: 9 sts.

Row 4: P2, K1, P3, K1, P2.

Row 5: K1, YO, knit across to marker, YO, slip marker, K1, YO, knit across to last st, YO, K1: 13 sts.

Row 6: P1, (K1, P1) across.

Row 7: K1, YO, knit across to marker, YO, slip marker, K1, YO, knit across to last st, YO, K1: 17 sts.

Row 8: P2, K1, (P1, K1) across to within 2 sts of marker, P3, K1, (P1, K1) across to last 2 sts, P2.

Repeat Rows 5-8 for pattern until Shawl measures approximately 72" (183 cm) across neck edge (end of rows) **or** to desired size, ending by working a **right** side row.

Last Row: Knit across.

Bind off all sts in **knit**.

Turn edge at neck to right side to form a collar.

Design by Cathy Hardy.

So Nice to Have You around

Finished Size: 22¹⁄₂" (57 cm) across top edge
18¹⁄₂" (47 cm) deep
59" (150 cm) across bottom edge

MATERIALS

Light Weight Variegated Yarn
[1.75 ounces, 200 yards
(50 grams, 182 meters) per skein]:
4 skeins
29" (73.5 cm) Circular knitting needle,
size 5 (3.75 mm) **or** size needed for gauge
Markers - 17
Decorative pin (for a closure)

GAUGE: In Stockinette Stitch,
26 sts and 36 rows = 4" (10 cm)

This Shawl begins at the neck edge and works down. The YO's double as increases and alternating vertical eyelets.

SHAWL

Cast on 145 sts.

Row 1: P1, (K1, P1) across.

Row 2 (Right side)**:** K1, (P1, K1) across.

Rows 3-8: Repeat Rows 1 and 2, 3 times.

Row 9: (P1, K1) twice, purl across to last 4 sts, (K1, P1) twice.

Row 10: (K1, P1) twice, knit across to last 4 sts, (P1, K1) twice.

Rows 11-17: Repeat Rows 9 and 10, 3 times; then repeat Row 9 once **more**.

Row 18 (Increase row)**:** (K1, P1) twice, K5, place marker *(see Markers, page 41)*, YO *(Fig. 8a, page 44)*, (K8, place marker, YO) across to last 8 sts, K4, (P1, K1) twice: 162 sts.

Rows 19-27: Repeat Rows 9 and 10, 4 times; then repeat Row 9 once **more**.

Row 28 (Increase row)**:** (K1, P1) twice, (knit across to marker, YO, slip marker) 17 times, knit across to last 4 sts, (P1, K1) twice: 179 sts.

Rows 29-37: Repeat Rows 9 and 10, 4 times; then repeat Row 9 once **more**.

Row 38 (Increase row)**:** (K1, P1) twice, (knit across to marker, K1, YO) 17 times, knit across to last 4 sts, (P1, K1) twice: 196 sts.

Rows 39-157: Repeat Rows 19-38, 5 times; then repeat Rows 19-37 once **more**: 383 sts.

Rows 158-165: P1, (K1, P1) across (for Seed St).

Bind off all sts in **pattern**.

Use a decorative pin as a closure.

Design by Cathy Hardy.

A Little Something for you

■■□□ EASY

Finished Size: 71¹/₂" wide x 36¹/₂" deep
(181.5 cm x 92.5 cm)

MATERIALS

Medium Weight Cotton Blend Yarn
[3.5 ounces, 178 yards
(100 grams, 163 meters) per skein]:
  6 skeins
29" (73.5 cm) Circular knitting needle,
  size 6 (4 mm) **or** size needed for gauge

GAUGE: In pattern,
    16 sts and 24 rows = 4" (10 cm)

Gauge Swatch: 5¹/₂"w x 4¹/₄"h (14 x 10.75 cm)
Cast on 22 sts.
Row 1 (Right side): Purl across.
Row 2: P1, K2, YO *(Fig. 8a, page 44)*, [slip 1 as
if to **knit**, K1, PSSO *(Figs. 12a & b, page 45)*],
★ P4, K2, YO, slip 1 as if to **knit**, K1, PSSO;
repeat from ★ once **more**, P1.
Row 3: P3, YO *(Fig. 8b, page 44)*, P2 tog
(Fig. 15, page 46), ★ K4, P2, YO, P2 tog; repeat
from ★ once **more**, P1.
Rows 4-25: Repeat Rows 2 and 3, 11 times.
Bind off all sts in **knit**.

This Shawl begins at the bottom tip and is
worked up. Shaping is achieved by adding on
stitches using the knit cast on method
(Figs. 5a-e, pages 42 & 43) in a stair-step
fashion.

SHAWL

Cast on 6 sts.

Row 1 (Right side): Purl across.

Row 2: P1, K2, YO *(Fig. 8a, page 44)*, [slip 1 as
if to **knit**, K1, PSSO *(Figs. 12a & b, page 45)*], P1.

Instructions continued on page 16.

Row 3: P3, YO *(Fig. 8b, page 44)*, P2 tog *(Fig. 15, page 46)*, P1.

Rows 4-6: Repeat Rows 2 and 3 once, then repeat Row 2 once **more**.

Row 7: Add on 4 sts, P7, YO, P2 tog, P1: 10 sts.

Row 8: Add on 4 sts, P1, K2, YO, slip 1 as if to **knit**, K1, PSSO, P4, K2, YO, slip 1 as if to **knit**, K1, PSSO, P1: 14 sts.

Row 9: P3, YO, P2 tog, K4, P2, YO, P2 tog, P1.

Row 10: P1, K2, YO, slip 1 as if to **knit**, K1, PSSO, P4, K2, YO, slip 1 as if to **knit**, K1, PSSO, P1.

Rows 11 and 12: Repeat Rows 9 and 10.

Row 13: Add on 4 sts, P7, YO, P2 tog, K4, P2, YO, P2 tog, P1: 18 sts.

Row 14: Add on 4 sts, P1, K2, YO, slip 1 as if to **knit**, K1, PSSO, ★ P4, K2, YO, slip 1 as if to **knit**, K1, PSSO; repeat from ★ across to last st, P1: 22 sts.

Row 15: P3, YO, P2 tog, ★ K4, P2, YO, P2 tog; repeat from ★ across to last st, P1.

Row 16: P1, K2, YO, slip 1 as if to **knit**, K1, PSSO, ★ P4, K2, YO, slip 1 as if to **knit**, K1, PSSO; repeat from ★ across to last st, P1.

Rows 17 and 18: Repeat Rows 15 and 16.

Row 19: Add on 4 sts, P7, YO, P2 tog, ★ K4, P2, YO, P2 tog; repeat from ★ across to last st, P1: 26 sts.

Repeat Rows 14-19 for pattern until Shawl measures approximately 71½" (181.5 cm) across top edge **or** to desired size, ending by working Row 18; then repeat Row 15 once **more**.

Last 4 Rows: Purl across.

Bind off all sts in **purl**.

Design by Cathy Hardy.

Thinking of you

◼◼◼◻ INTERMEDIATE

Finished Size: 16" x 57" (40.5 cm x 145 cm)
unblocked,
20" x 61" (51 cm x 155 cm)
blocked

MATERIALS
Light Weight Wool Blend Yarn
[1.75 ounces, 192 yards
(50 grams, 175 meters) per hank]:
  4 hanks
Straight knitting needles, size 8 (5 mm)
  or size needed for gauge
Pins for blocking

Note: A Wool blend was chosen to make this lacy shawl. It will stretch in the blocking process.

GAUGE: In Center Eyelet pattern,
      2 repeats (16 sts) and 21 rows =
      3½" (9 cm)

Gauge Swatch: 4¼"w x 4"h (10.75 cm x 10 cm)
Cast on 19 sts **loosely**.
Row 1: Purl across.
Row 2: K3, ★ K2 tog *(Fig. 9, page 45)*, YO *(Fig. 8a, page 44)*, K1, YO, SSK *(Figs. 14a-c, page 46)*, K3; repeat from ★ once **more**.
Rows 3-24: Repeat Rows 1 and 2, 11 times.
Bind off all sts in **purl**.

This Shawl begins with the Edging, which is worked as long as the finished width. Stitches will be picked up along one edge and worked across the width. For the second Edging, stitches will be cast on and worked the same as the first Edging, joining one stitch of the Body at the end of every other row.

This Shawl can be made following written instructions or by following the Charts on page 21 *(see Charts, page 41)*. Choose whichever is easiest for you.

EDGING
Cast on 17 sts **loosely**.

Foundation Row: K5, P 10, K2.

Row 1 (Right side)**:** Slip 1 as if to **knit**, (K2 tog, YO) twice *(Fig. 9, page 45 and Fig. 8a, page 44)*, K2, SSK *(Figs. 14a-c, page 46)*, K1, (K2 tog, YO) twice, K3: 16 sts.

Row 2: Slip 1 as if to **knit**, K2 tog, YO, K3, P8, K2.

Row 3: Slip 1 as if to **knit**, K1, YO, K2 tog, YO, K1, YO, K2, SSK, (K2 tog, YO) twice, K3: 17 sts.

Row 4: Slip 1 as if to **knit**, K2 tog, YO, K3, P9, K2.

Row 5: Slip 1 as if to **knit**, K1, YO, K2 tog, (YO, K3) twice, (K2 tog, YO) twice, K3: 19 sts.

Instructions continued on page 18.

Row 6: Slip 1 as if to **knit**, K2 tog, YO, K3, P 11, K2.

Row 7: Slip 1 as if to **knit**, K1, YO, K2 tog, YO, K5, YO, K3, (K2 tog, YO) twice, K3: 21 sts.

Row 8: Slip 1 as if to **knit**, K2 tog, YO, K3, P 13, K2.

Row 9: Slip 1 as if to **knit**, (K2 tog, YO) twice, K2, [slip 1 as if to **knit**, K2 tog, PSSO *(Fig. 13, page 45)*], K4, (K2 tog, YO) twice, K3: 19 sts.

Row 10: Slip 1 as if to **knit**, K2 tog, YO, K3, P 11, K2.

Row 11: Slip 1 as if to **knit**, (K2 tog, YO) twice, K2, SSK, K3, (K2 tog, YO) twice, K3: 18 sts.

Row 12: Slip 1 as if to **knit**, K2 tog, YO, K3, P 10, K2.

Row 13: Slip 1 as if to **knit**, (K2 tog, YO) twice, K2, SSK, K2, (K2 tog, YO) twice, K3: 17 sts.

Row 14: Slip 1 as if to **knit**, K2 tog, YO, K3, P9, K2.

Rows 15-114: Repeat Rows 1-14, 7 times; then repeat Rows 1 and 2 once **more**.

Bind off all sts **loosely** in knit, leaving last st on needle; do **not** cut yarn.

CENTER EYELET PANEL

With **right** side of Edging facing, pick up 74 sts evenly spaced across end of rows *(Fig. 17, page 47)*: 75 sts.

Foundation Row: K4, purl across to last 4 sts, K4.

Row 1: Slip 1 as if to **knit**, K1, K2 tog, YO, K3, K2 tog, YO, ★ K1, YO, SSK, K3, K2 tog, YO; repeat from ★ across to last 2 sts, K2.

Row 2: Slip 1 as if to **knit**, K1, K2 tog, YO *(Fig. 8c, page 44)*, purl across to last 4 sts, K2 tog, YO, K2.

Repeat Rows 1 and 2 for pattern until Shawl measures approximately 54" (137 cm), ending by working Row 2.

Next Row: Slip 1 as if to **knit**, knit across.

Last Row: K3, K2 tog, (P2, P2 tog) 16 times *(Fig. 15, page 46)*, P1, K2 tog, K3: 57 sts.

EDGING

Add on 17 sts onto working needle *(Figs. 5a-e, pages 42 & 43)*: 74 sts.

Row 1: Slip 1 as if to **knit**, (K2 tog, YO) twice, K2, SSK, K1, (K2 tog, YO) twice, K2, knit last st of Edging and next st of Panel together, leave remaining sts on left-hand needle unworked: 16 sts on right-hand needle.

Row 2: Turn; K1, K2 tog, YO, K3, P8, K2.

Row 3: Slip 1 as if to **knit**, K1, YO, K2 tog, YO, K1, YO, K2, SSK, (K2 tog, YO) twice, K2, knit last st of Edging and next st of Panel together: 17 sts on right-hand needle.

Row 4: Turn; K1, K2 tog, YO, K3, P9, K2.

Row 5: Slip 1 as if to **knit**, K1, YO, K2 tog, (YO, K3) twice, (K2 tog, YO) twice, K2, knit last st of Edging and next st of Panel together: 19 sts on right-hand needle.

Row 6: Turn; K1, K2 tog, YO, K3, P 11, K2.

Instructions continued on page 20

Row 7: Slip 1 as if to **knit**, K1, YO, K2 tog, YO, K5, YO, K3, (K2 tog, YO) twice, K2, knit last st of Edging and next st of Panel together: 21 sts on right-hand needle.

Row 8: Turn; K1, K2 tog, YO, K3, P 13, K2.

Row 9: Slip 1 as if to **knit**, (K2 tog, YO) twice, K2, slip 1 as if to **knit**, K2 tog, PSSO, K4, (K2 tog, YO) twice, K2, knit last st of Edging and next st of Panel together: 19 sts on right-hand needle.

Row 10: Turn; K1, K2 tog, YO, K3, P 11, K2.

Row 11: Slip 1 as if to **knit**, (K2 tog, YO) twice, K2, SSK, K3, (K2 tog, YO) twice, K2, knit last st of Edging and next st of Panel together: 18 sts on right-hand needle.

Row 12: Turn; K1, K2 tog, YO, K3, P 10, K2.

Row 13: Slip 1 as if to **knit**, (K2 tog, YO) twice, K2, SSK, K2, (K2 tog, YO) twice, K2, knit last st of Edging and next st of Panel together: 17 sts on right-hand needle.

Row 14: Turn; K1, K2 tog, YO, K3, P9, K2.

Repeat Rows 1-14 until all sts on the Center Eyelet Panel are used, ending by working Row 1.

Bind off all sts **loosely** in pattern.

Wash and block Shawl *(see Blocking, page 47)*.

Design by Kay Meadors.

CHART INSTRUCTIONS

EDGING

Cast on 17 sts **loosely**.
Foundation Row: K5, P 10, K2.
Rows 1-114: Follow chart 1 Rows 1-14, 8 times; then repeat Rows 1 and 2 once **more**.
Bind off all sts **loosely** in knit, leaving last st on needle; do **not** cut yarn.

EDGING

Add on 17 sts onto working needle (*Figs. 5a-e, pages 42 & 43*): 74 sts.
Follow chart 3 Rows 1-14 until all sts on the Center Eyelet Panel are used, ending by working Row 1.
Bind off all sts **loosely** in pattern.

Wash and block Shawl (*see Blocking, page 47*).

CHART 1

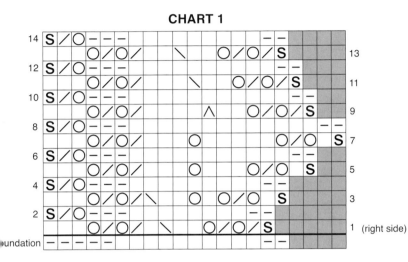

CHART 3

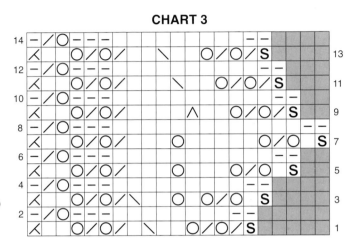

CENTER EYELET PANEL

With **right** side of Edging facing, pick up 74 sts evenly spaced across end of rows (*Fig. 17, page 47*): 75 sts.
Foundation Row: K4, purl across to last 4 sts, K4.
Follow chart 2 Rows 1 and 2 until Shawl measures approximately 54" (137 cm), ending by working Row 2.
Next Row: Slip 1 as if to **knit**, knit across.
Last Row: K3, K2 tog, (P2, P2 tog) 16 times (*Fig. 15, page 46*), P1, K2 tog, K3: 57 sts.

CHART 2

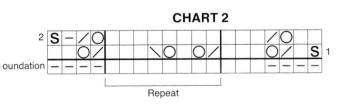

Repeat

KEY

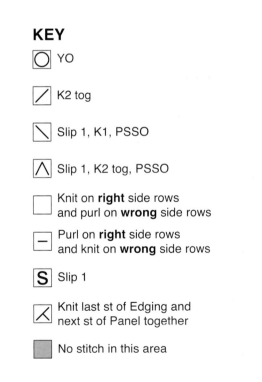

○ YO

╱ K2 tog

╲ Slip 1, K1, PSSO

⋀ Slip 1, K2 tog, PSSO

☐ Knit on **right** side rows and purl on **wrong** side rows

⊟ Purl on **right** side rows and knit on **wrong** side rows

S Slip 1

⊠ Knit last st of Edging and next st of Panel together

▨ No stitch in this area

Gifts to share

Finished Size: 72" wide x 36" deep
(183 cm x 91.5 cm)

MATERIALS
Medium Weight Yarn
[2.8 ounces, 145 yards
(80 grams, 133 meters) per skein]:
    Green - 7 skeins
    Lt Green - 4 skeins
29" (73.5 cm) Circular knitting needle,
    size 8 (5 mm) **or** size needed for gauge
Markers

GAUGE: 20 sts = 4" (10 cm)
        In Woven Pattern, 20 rows = 2½"
        (6.25 cm) measured across end of rows

Gauge Swatch: 2¼"h x 5¾" across bottom
edge (5.75 cm x 14.5 cm)
Work Woven Pattern through Row 15.

This Shawl begins at the center of the neck and is worked down. The end of rows form the neck edge and the Make One increases form the triangular shape.

WOVEN PATTERN
With Green, cast on 5 sts.

Row 1: P3, place marker *(see Markers, page 41)*, P2.

Note: Always work the center M1 *(Figs. 7a & b, page 44)* **before** slipping the marker.

Row 2 (Right side): K1, (M1, K1) across: 9 sts.

Tip: When working the stitch after a slipped stitch, hold the yarn with even tension so the piece lies flat and doesn't pucker.

Row 3: P1, (with yarn in **back** slip 1 as if to **purl**, P1) across.

Note: When working a M1 before a slipped stitch, insert the left needle under the strand that is carried in front of the next stitch.

Row 4 (Increase row): K1, M1, knit across to marker, M1, K1, M1, knit across to last st, M1, K1: 13 sts.

Instructions continued on page 24.

Rows 5-34: Repeat Rows 3 and 4, 15 times: 73 sts.

Do **not** cut Green; carry unused color along edge.

Rows 35 and 36: With Lt Green, repeat Rows 3 and 4: 77 sts.

Rows 37 and 38: With Green, repeat Rows 3 and 4: 81 sts.

Rows 39-76: Repeat Rows 35-38, 9 times; then with Lt Green repeat Rows 3 and 4 once **more**: 157 sts.

Cut Green only.

KNOT PATTERN

Row 1: With Lt Green, knit across.

Row 2 (Increase row): K1, M1, knit across to marker, M1, K1, M1, knit across to last st, M1, K1: 161 sts.

Row 3: (P1, with yarn in **back** slip 1 as if to **purl**) twice, purl across to last 4 sts, (with yarn in **back** slip 1 as if to **purl**, P1) twice.

To work Knot (uses 3 sts):
P3 tog leaving sts on needle **(Fig. 16, page 46)**, knit same 3 sts together again leaving sts on left needle **(Fig. 11, page 45)**, then purl same 3 sts together again slipping sts off left needle.

Row 4 (Increase row): K1, M1, K4, work Knot, (K3, work Knot) across to marker, M1, K1, M1, work Knot, (K3, work Knot) across to last 5 sts, K4, M1, K1: 165 sts.

Rows 5-9: Repeat Row 3, then repeat Rows 2 and 3 twice: 173 sts.

Rows 10-53: Repeat Rows 4-9, 7 times; then repeat Rows 4 and 5 once **more**: 261 sts.

Do **not** cut Lt Green.

Row 54: With Green, K1, M1, knit across to marker, M1, K1, M1, knit across to last st, M1, K1: 265 sts.

Row 55: Knit across.

Row 56: With Lt Green, K1, M1, knit across to marker, M1, K1, M1, knit across to last st, M1, K1: 269 sts.

Row 57: Knit across; cut Lt Green.

EYELET PATTERN

Row 1 (Increase row)**:** With Green, K1, M1, knit across to marker, M1, K1, M1, knit across to last st, M1, K1: 273 sts.

Row 2: (P1, with yarn in **back** slip 1 as if to **purl**) twice, purl across to last 4 sts, (with yarn in **back** slip 1 as if to **purl**, P1) twice.

Rows 3 and 4: Repeat Rows 1 and 2: 277 sts.

Row 5: K1, M1, K7, K2 tog **(Fig. 9, page 45)**, YO **(Fig. 8a, page 44)**, K3, YO, [slip 1 as if to **knit**, K1, PSSO **(Figs. 12a & b, page 45)**], † K5, K2 tog, YO, K3, YO, slip 1 as if to **knit**, K1, PSSO †, repeat from † to † across to within 3 sts of marker, K3, M1, K1, M1, K3, K2 tog, YO, K3, YO, slip 1 as if to **knit**, K1, PSSO, repeat from † to † across to last 8 sts, K7, M1, K1: 281 sts.

Row 6: (P1, with yarn in **back** slip 1 as if to **purl**) twice, purl across to last 4 sts, (with yarn in **back** slip 1 as if to **purl**, P1) twice.

Row 7: K1, M1, K 10, YO, [slip 1 as if to **knit**, K2 tog, PSSO **(Fig. 13, page 45)**], YO, † K9, YO, slip 1 as if to **knit**, K2 tog, PSSO, YO †, repeat from † to † across to within 6 sts of marker, K6, M1, K1, M1, K6, YO, slip 1 as if to **knit**, K2 tog, PSSO, YO, repeat from † to † across to last 11 sts, K 10, M1, K1: 285 sts.

Rows 8-16: Repeat Row 2, then repeat Rows 1 and 2, 4 times: 301 sts.

Repeat Rows 5-16 for pattern until Shawl measures approximately 66" (167.5 cm) across neck edge (end of rows) **or** to desired size, ending by working Row 11.

Last 2 Rows: With Lt Green, purl across.

Do **not** cut yarns.

WOVEN PATTERN
Row 1: With Lt Green, P1, (with yarn in **back** slip 1 as if to **purl**, P1) across.

Row 2 (Increase row): K1, M1, knit across to marker, M1, K1, M1, knit across to last st, M1, K1.

Rows 3 and 4: With Green, repeat Rows 1 and 2.

Repeat Rows 1-4 until Shawl measures approximately 70" (178 cm) across neck edge, ending by working Row 2; do **not** cut yarns.

EDGING
Rows 1 and 2: With Green, purl across.

Rows 3 and 4: With Lt Green, purl across.

Cut Lt Green.

Rows 5 and 6: With Green, purl across.

Bind off all sts in **purl**.

Design by Cathy Hardy.

A Wisp of warmth

Finished Size: Unblocked 55" (139.5 cm) diameter, blocked 70" (178 cm)

MATERIALS

Super Fine Wool Yarn [1.75 ounces, 440 yards (50 grams, 402 meters) per hank]: 4 hanks

Set of four, 8" (20.5 cm) double pointed knitting needles, size 6 (4 mm) **or** size needed for gauge

16" (40.5 cm), 24" (61 cm) and 36" (91.5 cm) Circular knitting needles, size 6 (4 mm) **or** size needed for gauge

Split ring marker

Markers

Pins for blocking

Note: Wool was chosen to make this lacy shawl. It will help it stretch during the blocking process.

GAUGE: In Stockinette Stitch, 24 sts = 4" (10 cm)

This Shawl is worked in rounds, forming a large circle. You will begin using double pointed needles and change to a circular needle when the stitches become crowded.

The charts, page 29, can be used along with the instructions *(see Charts, page 41).*

SHAWL

Cast 9 sts loosely onto a double pointed needle; transfer 3 sts onto each of 2 other double pointed needles *(see Double Pointed Needles, page 41)*: 3 sts each needle (9 sts total).

Note: Place a split ring marker at the beginning of the first cast on stitch to mark the beginning of the round. Begin working in rounds, making sure that the first round is not twisted.

Rnd 1: Knit across each needle.

Note: If there is a YO at the end of each needle, take care not to drop it.

Instructions continued on page 28.

Rnd 2: (K1, YO) across each needle *(Fig. 8a, page 44)*: 6 sts on each needle (18 sts total).

Rnds 3-5: Knit across each needle.

Rnd 6: (K1, YO) across each needle: 12 sts on each needle (36 sts total).

Rnds 7-9: Knit across each needle.

Rnd 10: (K2 tog, YO) across each needle *(Fig. 9, page 45)*.

Rnds 11-13: Knit across each needle.

Rnd 14: (K1, YO) across each needle: 24 sts on each needle (72 sts total).

Rnds 15 and 16: Knit across each needle.

Rnd 17: (K 12, M1, K 12) across each needle *(Figs. 7a & b, page 44)*: 25 sts on each needle (75 sts total).

Rnd 18: Knit across each needle.

Rnd 19: ★ K2 tog, YO, K1, YO, SSK *(Figs. 14a-c, page 46)*; repeat from ★ across each needle.

Rnd 20: Knit across each needle.

Rnds 21-23: Repeat Rnds 19 and 20 once, then repeat Rnd 19 once **more**.

Rnds 24-27: Knit across each needle.

Note: At this point you may be able to replace the double pointed needles with a 16" (40.5 cm) circular needle. When working the next round, place markers as indicated (see Markers, page 41), making sure that the beginning marker is a different color or type to mark the beginning of the rounds. Instructions will now reflect that change by working around.

Rnd 28: (K1, YO) around placing a marker after every 30 sts: 30 sts in each of 5 sections (150 sts total).

Rnds 29-32: Knit around.

Rnd 33: ★ K2 tog, YO, K1, YO, SSK; repeat from ★ around.

Rnd 34: Knit around.

Rnds 35-37: Repeat Rnds 33 and 34 once, then repeat Rnd 33 once **more**.

Rnds 38-41: Knit around.

Rnd 42: (K2 tog, YO) around.

Rnds 43-55: Repeat Rnds 29-41.

Rnd 56: (K1, YO) around: 60 sts in each section (300 sts total).

Rnds 57-111: Repeat Rnds 29-42, 3 times; then repeat Rnds 29-41 once **more**.

Rnd 112: (K1, YO) around placing additional markers to have a marker every 60 sts: 60 sts in each of 10 sections (600 sts total).

Rnds 113-204: Repeat Rnds 29-42, 6 times; then repeat Rnds 29-36 once **more**.

Rnd 205: ★ K2 tog, YO, K1, YO, SSK, YO; repeat from ★ around: 72 sts in each section (720 sts total).

Bind off all sts as follows: K2, return the 2 sts just knit back onto left needle, knit these 2 sts together through back loop *(Fig. 10, page 45)*, ★ K1, return the 2 sts on right needle back onto left needle, knit these 2 sts together through back loop; repeat from ★ across; finish off.

Wash and block Shawl *(see Blocking, page 47)*.

Design by Kay Meadors.

CHART

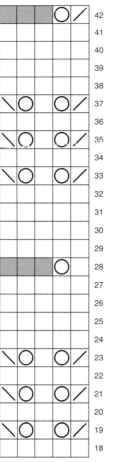

Repeat

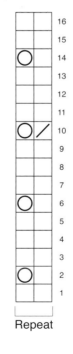

Repeat

KEY

- ◯ YO
- ╱ K2 tog
- ╲ SSK
- ☐ Knit
- ▨ No stitch in this area

A Girl's Best friend

 **INTERMEDIATE**

Finished Size: 25" x 70" (63.5 cm x 178 cm)

MATERIALS
Medium Weight Yarn **4** MEDIUM
[5 ounces, 256 yards
(140 grams, 234 meters) per skein]:
  6 skeins
29" (73.5 cm) Circular knitting needle,
  size 9 (5.5 mm) **or** size needed for gauge
Cable needle

GAUGE: In Stockinette Stitch,
     16 sts and 22 rows = 4" (10 cm)

This Shawl can be made following written instructions or by following the Charts on pages 34 and 35 *(see Charts, page 41)*. Choose whichever is easiest for you.

Each row is worked across the length of the Shawl.

CABLE (uses 7 sts)
Slip next 3 sts onto cable needle and hold in **front** of work, K4 from left needle, K3 from cable needle.

SHAWL
Cast on 281 sts.

Rows 1-5: Purl across.

Row 6 (Right side)**:** P3, K2 tog *(Fig. 9, page 45)*, YO *(Fig. 8a, page 44)*, (K2 tog, YO) across to last 4 sts, K1, P3.

Rows 7-9: Purl across.

Row 10: P3, knit across to last 3 sts, P3.

Row 11 AND ALL WRONG SIDE ROWS: Purl across.

Row 12: P3, K9, YO, [slip 1 as if to **knit**, K1, PSSO *(Figs. 12a & b, page 45)*], ★ K 14, YO, slip 1 as if to **knit**, K1, PSSO; repeat from ★ across to last 11 sts, K8, P3.

Instructions continued on page 32.

Row 14: P3, K7, K2 tog, YO, K1, YO, slip 1 as if to **knit**, K1, PSSO, ★ K 11, K2 tog, YO, K1, YO, slip 1 as if to **knit**, K1, PSSO; repeat from ★ across to last 10 sts, K7, P3.

Row 16: P3, K6, K2 tog, YO, K3, YO, slip 1 as if to **knit**, K1, PSSO, ★ K9, K2 tog, YO, K3, YO, slip 1 as if to **knit**, K1, PSSO; repeat from ★ across to last 9 sts, K6, P3.

Row 18: P3, K5, K2 tog, YO, K5, YO, slip 1 as if to **knit**, K1, PSSO, ★ K7, K2 tog, YO, K5, YO, slip 1 as if to **knit**, K1, PSSO; repeat from ★ across to last 8 sts, K5, P3.

Row 20: P3, K4, K2 tog, YO, K7, YO, slip 1 as if to **knit**, K1, PSSO, ★ K5, K2 tog, YO, K7, YO, slip 1 as if to **knit**, K1, PSSO; repeat from ★ across to last 7 sts, K4, P3.

Row 22: P3, K4, slip 1 as if to **knit**, K1, PSSO, YO, work Cable, YO, K2 tog, ★ K5, slip 1 as if to **knit**, K1, PSSO, YO, work Cable, YO, K2 tog; repeat from ★ across to last 7 sts, K4, P3.

Row 24: P3, K4, YO, slip 1 as if to **knit**, K1, PSSO, K7, K2 tog, YO, ★ K5, YO, slip 1 as if to **knit**, K1, PSSO, K7, K2 tog, YO; repeat from ★ across to last 7 sts, K4, P3.

Row 26: P3, K5, YO, slip 1 as if to **knit**, K1, PSSO, K5, K2 tog, YO, ★ K7, YO, slip 1 as if to **knit**, K1, PSSO, K5, K2 tog, YO; repeat from ★ across to last 8 sts, K5, P3.

Row 28: P3, K6, YO, slip 1 as if to **knit**, K1, PSSO, K3, K2 tog, YO, ★ K9, YO, slip 1 as if to **knit**, K1, PSSO, K3, K2 tog, YO; repeat from ★ across to last 9 sts, K6, P3.

Row 30: P3, K7, YO, slip 1 as if to **knit**, K1, PSSO, K1, K2 tog, YO, ★ K 11, YO, slip 1 as if to **knit**, K1, PSSO, K1, K2 tog, YO; repeat from ★ across to last 10 sts, K7, P3.

Row 32: P3, K8, YO, [slip 1 as if to **knit**, K2 tog, PSSO *(Fig. 13, page 45)*] , YO, ★ K 13, YO, slip 1 as if to **knit**, K2 tog, PSSO, YO; repeat from ★ across to last 11 sts, K8, P3.

Row 34: P3, knit across to last 3 sts, P3.

Row 36: Purl across.

Row 38: P3, (K2 tog, YO) across to last 4 sts, K1, P3.

Row 40: Purl across.

Row 42: P3, knit across to last 3 sts, P3.

Row 44: P3, K4, YO, slip 1 as if to **knit**, K1, PSSO, ★ K 12, YO, slip 1 as if to **knit**, K1, PSSO; repeat from ★ across to last 6 sts, K3, P3.

Row 46: P3, K2, K2 tog, YO, K1, YO, slip 1 as if to **knit**, K1, PSSO, ★ K9, K2 tog, YO, K1, YO, slip 1 as if to **knit**, K1, PSSO; repeat from ★ across to last 5 sts, K2, P3.

Row 48: P3, K1, K2 tog, YO, K3, YO, slip 1 as if to **knit**, K1, PSSO, ★ K7, K2 tog, YO, K3, YO, slip 1 as if to **knit**, K1, PSSO; repeat from ★ across to last 4 sts, K1, P3.

Row 50: P3, K3, YO, slip 1 as if to **knit**, K2 tog, PSSO, YO, ★ K 11, YO, slip 1 as if to **knit**, K2 tog, PSSO, YO; repeat from ★ across to last 6 sts, K3, P3.

Row 52: P3, K4, YO, slip 1 as if to **knit**, K1, PSSO, ★ K 12, YO, slip 1 as if to **knit**, K1, PSSO; repeat from ★ across to last 6 sts, K3, P3.

Row 54: P3, K 11, YO, slip 1 as if to **knit**, K1, PSSO, ★ K 12, YO, slip 1 as if to **knit**, K1, PSSO; repeat from ★ across to last 13 sts, K 10, P3.

Row 56: P3, K9, ★ K2 tog, YO, K1, YO, slip 1 as if to **knit**, K1, PSSO, K9; repeat from ★ across to last 3 sts, P3.

Row 58: P3, K8, K2 tog, YO, K3, YO, slip 1 as if to **knit**, K1, PSSO, ★ K7, K2 tog, YO, K3, YO, slip 1 as if to **knit**, K1, PSSO; repeat from ★ across to last 11 sts, K8, P3.

Row 60: P3, K 10, YO, slip 1 as if to **knit**, K2 tog, PSSO, YO, ★ K 11, YO, slip 1 as if to **knit**, K2 tog, PSSO, YO; repeat from ★ across to last 13 sts, K 10, P3.

Row 62: P3, K11, YO, slip 1 as if to **knit**, K1, PSSO, ★ K 12, YO, slip 1 as if to **knit**, K1, PSSO; repeat from ★ across to last 13 sts, K 10, P3.

Rows 64-113: Repeat Rows 44-63 twice, then repeat Rows 44-53 once **more**.

Rows 114-123: Repeat Rows 34-43.

Rows 124-150: Repeat Rows 12-38.

Rows 151-155: Purl across.

Bind off all sts in **purl**.

Design by Cathy Hardy.

CHART INSTRUCTIONS

Cast on 281 sts.

Rows 1-43: Follow chart.

Rows 44-113: Follow chart Rows 44-63, 3 times; then repeat Rows 44-53 once **more**.

Rows 114-123: Repeat Rows 34-43.

Rows 124-150: Repeat Rows 12-38.

Rows 151-155: Purl across.

Bind off all sts in **purl**.

KEY

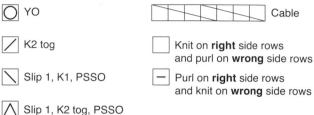

◯	YO
╱	K2 tog
╲	Slip 1, K1, PSSO
∧	Slip 1, K2 tog, PSSO

Cable

☐ Knit on **right** side rows and purl on **wrong** side rows

— Purl on **right** side rows and knit on **wrong** side rows

CHART

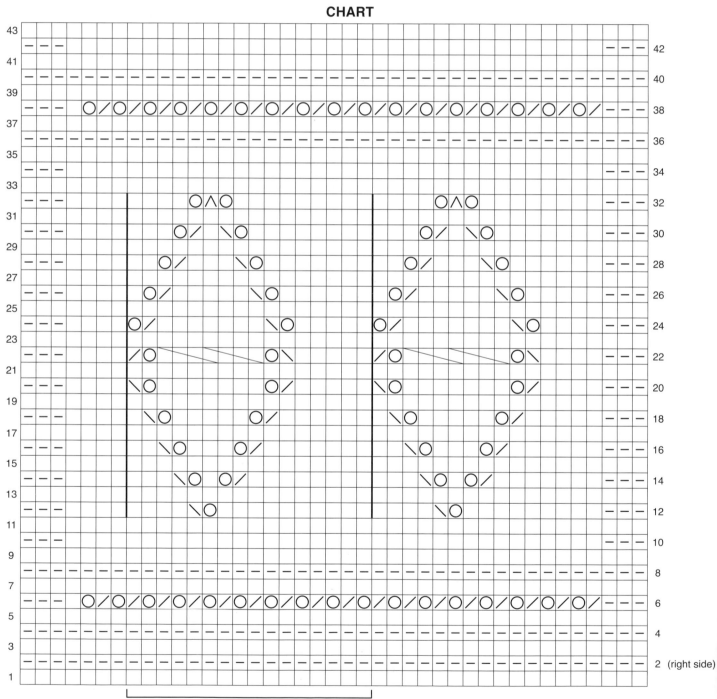

Repeat

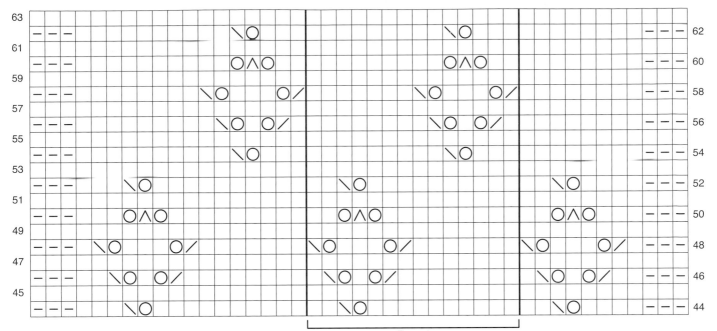

Repeat

Always With you

INTERMEDIATE

Finished Size: 20" x 72" (51 cm x 183 cm)

MATERIALS

Medium Weight Yarn
[3.5 ounces, 170 yards
(100 grams, 156 meters) per skein]:
   Rose - 5 skeins
   Purple - 2 skeins
[3.5 ounces, 210 yards
(100 grams, 192 meters) per skein]:
   Brown - 1 skein
Straight knitting needles, size 8 (5 mm)
   or size needed for gauge
29" (73.5 cm) Circular knitting needle,
   size 8 (5 mm) **or** size needed for gauge
Cable needle

GAUGES: Cable Panel = 3" (7.5 cm) wide
and 16 rows = $2^3/_4$" (7 cm);
Patterns 1, 3, & 4: 18 sts = 4" (10 cm);
Pattern 2, 18 sts = $3^1/_2$" (9 cm)

Gauge Swatch - Pattern 1: 4" (10 cm) square
With Rose cast on 18 sts.
Rows 1-3: Knit across.
Row 4: ★ P3 tog leaving sts on needle
(Fig. 16, page 46), YO **(Fig. 8b, page 44)**, purl
same 3 sts together again slipping sts off left
needle; repeat from ★ across.
Rows 5-23: Repeat Rows 1-4, 4 times; then
repeat Rows 1-3 once **more**.
Bind off all sts in **knit**.

This Shawl begins with the cable pattern, which
is worked to the finished length. Stitches will
be picked up along one long edge and worked
across to the finished width.

CABLE PANEL

With straight needles and Rose, cast on 15 sts.

Rows 1-3: Knit across.

Row 4: K8, M1 **(Figs. 7a & b, page 44)**, K1, M1,
K6: 17 sts.

When working with Purple or Brown, carry
Rose loosely on the wrong side.

Instructions continued on page 38.

Row 6: P1, K1, P2, K3, P5, K3, P1, K1.

To work Cable (uses 5 sts): Slip next 3 sts onto cable needle and hold in **front** of work, K2 from left needle, slip Rose st from cable needle back onto left needle and knit it, K2 from cable needle.

Row 7: P1, K1, P3, work Cable, P3, (K1, P1) twice.

Row 8: P1, K1, P2, K3, P5, K3, P1, K1.

Row 9: P1, K1, P3, K5, P3, (K1, P1) twice.

Row 10: P1, K1, P2, K3, P5, K3, P1, K1.

Row 11: P1, K1, P3, K2, (K, P, K, P, K) **all** in next st, pass second, third, fourth, and fifth sts on right needle over first st, K2, P3, (K1, P1) twice.

Row 12: P1, K1, P2, K3, P5, K3, P1, K1.

Row 13: P1, K1, P3, K5, P3, (K1, P1) twice.

Row 14: P1, K1, P2, K3, P5, K3, P1, K1.

Repeat Rows 7-14 for pattern until Panel measures approximately 71½" (181.5 cm) from cast on edge, ending by working Row 8.

Cut Purple and Brown.

Next Row: With Rose, K5, [slip 1 as if to **knit**, K1, PSSO *(Figs. 12a & b, page 45)*], K1, K2 tog *(Fig. 9, page 45)*, K7: 15 sts.

Last 3 Rows: Knit across.

Bind off all sts in **knit**.

PATTERN 1
With **right** side facing, using circular needle and Purple, and beginning at cast on edge, pick up and knit 324 sts evenly spaced across right edge of Cable Panel *(Fig. 17, page 47)*.

Row 1: Knit across; do **not** cut Purple.

Row 5 (Right side): P1, K1, P3, with Brown K2, with Rose K1, with Purple K2, with Rose P3, (K1, P1) twice.

Maintain colors on established stitches throughout Cable Panel.

When changing colors, always pick up the new color yarn from **beneath** the dropped yarn and keep the color which has just been worked to the left of it *(Fig. 3, page 41)*. This will prevent holes in the finished piece. Take extra care to keep your tension even.

Row 2: With Rose, knit across.

Row 3: K3, ★ P3 tog leaving sts on needle *(Fig. 16, page 46)*, YO *(Fig. 8b, page 44)*, purl same 3 sts together again slipping sts off left needle; repeat from ★ across to last 3 sts, K3.

Rows 4 and 5: With Purple, knit across.

Repeat Rows 2-5 for pattern until Pattern 1 measures approximately 8" (20.5 cm), ending by working Row 5.

Cut Purple; do **not** cut Rose.

PATTERN 2
Row 1: With Rose, K8, M1, (K7, M1) across to last 8 sts, K8: 369 sts.

Row 2: K3, (P3, K3) across.

To work Right Twist (uses 3 sts): Working in **front** of the piece, knit the third st on the left needle without slipping it off *(Fig. 1)*, then knit the first 2 sts on the left needle slipping all 3 sts off the left needle.

Fig. 1

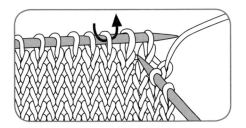

Row 3: With Rose, K3, (work Right Twist, K3) across.

Row 4: K3, (P3, K3) across.

Rows 5 and 6: With Brown, K3, (slip 3, K3) across.

Repeat Rows 3-6 for pattern until Pattern 2 measures approximately 6" (15 cm), ending by working Row 6.

Cut Brown.

Last 4 Rows: Repeat Rows 3 and 4 twice.

Do **not** cut Rose.

PATTERN 3
Row 1: With Purple, (K6, K2 tog) 4 times, K5, ★ K2 tog, K6, K2 tog, K5; repeat from ★ across to last 32 sts, (K2 tog, K6) 4 times: 321 sts.

Row 2: Knit across.

Row 3: With Brown, knit across.

Row 4: K3, ★ P3 tog leaving sts on needle, YO, purl same 3 sts together again slipping sts off left needle; repeat from ★ across to last 3 sts, K3.

Rows 5 and 6: With Purple, knit across.

Row 7: With Rose, knit across.

Row 8: Purl across.

Rows 9 and 10: With Purple, knit across.

Rows 11-15: Repeat Rows 3-7.

Cut Brown and Purple.

PATTERN 4
Rows 1-6: K3, P1, (K1, P1) across to last 3 sts, K3.

Bind off all sts in pattern.

Design by Cathy Hardy.

General instructions

ABBREVIATIONS

cm	centimeters
K	knit
M1	make one
mm	millimeters
P	purl
PSSO	pass slipped stitch(es) over
Rnd(s)	round(s)
SSK	slip, slip, knit
st(s)	stitch(es)
tog	together
YO	yarn over

★ — work instructions following ★ as many **more** times as indicated in addition to the first time.

† to † — work all instructions from first † to second † **as many** times as specified.

( ) or [ ] — work enclosed instructions **as many** times as specified by the number immediately following **or** work all enclosed instructions in the stitch indicated **or** contains explanatory remarks.

colon (:) — the number given after a colon at the end of a row or round denotes the number of stitches you should have on that row or round.

GAUGE

Exact gauge is **essential** for proper size. Before beginning your Shawl, make a sample swatch in the yarn and needle specified in the individual instructions. After completing the swatch, measure it, counting your stitches and rows carefully. If your swatch is larger or smaller than specified, **make another, changing needle size to get the correct gauge.** Keep trying until you find the size needles that will give you the specified gauge.

KNIT TERMINOLOGY	
UNITED STATES	INTERNATIONAL
gauge =	tension
bind off =	cast off
yarn over (YO) =	yarn forward (yfwd) **or** yarn around needle (yrn)

Yarn Weight Symbol & Names	SUPER FINE 1	FINE 2	LIGHT 3	MEDIUM 4	BULKY 5	SUPER BULKY 6
Type of Yarns in Category	Sock, Fingering Baby	Sport, Baby	DK, Light Worsted	Worsted, Afghan, Aran	Chunky, Craft, Rug	Bulky, Roving
Knit Gauge Ranges in Stockinette St to 4" (10 cm)	27-32 sts	23-26 sts	21-24 sts	16-20 sts	12-15 sts	6-11 sts
Advised Needle Size Range	1-3	3-5	5-7	7-9	9-11	11 and larger

■□□□ BEGINNER	Projects for first-time knitters using basic knit and purl stitches. Minimal shaping.
■■□□ EASY	Projects using basic stitches, repetitive stitch patterns, simple color changes, and simple shaping and finishing.
■■■□ INTERMEDIATE	Projects with a variety of stitches, such as basic cables and lace, simple intarsia, double-pointed needles and knitting in the round needle techniques, mid-level shaping and finishing.
■■■■ EXPERIENCED	Projects using advanced techniques and stitches, such as short rows, fair isle, more intricate intarsia, cables, lace patterns, and numerous color changes.

KNITTING NEEDLES															
U.S.	0	1	2	3	4	5	6	7	8	9	10	10½	11	13	15	17
U.K.	13	12	11	10	9	8	7	6	5	4	3	2	1	00	000	---
Metric - mm	2	2.25	2.75	3.25	3.5	3.75	4	4.5	5	5.5	6	6.5	8	9	10	12.75

MARKERS

As a convenience to you, we have used markers to mark the placement of increases and the beginning of rounds. Place markers as instructed. You may use purchased markers or tie a length of contrasting color yarn around the needle. When you reach a marker on each row or round, slip it from the left needle to the right needle; remove it when no longer needed.

CHARTS

You might find following a chart easier than following written instructions, as you can see what the pattern looks like and you can also see each row at a glance. If you've never followed a chart before, you can refer to the chart while you read the instructions until you are comfortable following a chart.

The chart shows each stitch as a square. Refer to the key given with each chart for a symbol guide of the stitches used.

Visualize the chart as your fabric, beginning at the bottom edge and looking at the right side. On the charts with a pattern repeat, it is indicated by a heavy vertical line and a bracketed indication. This section is to be repeated across the row. There are extra stitches on each side of the repeat.

When working in rounds, always follow the chart from **right** to **left**. When working in rows, on **right** side rows, follow the chart from **right** to **left**; on **wrong** side rows, follow the chart from **left** to **right**.

The first right side row is indicated and the row numbers are placed at the beginning of each row.

For ease in following the chart, place a ruler on the chart above the row being worked to help keep your place.

DOUBLE POINTED NEEDLES

Cast on the number of stitches indicated. Divide the stitches evenly between three double pointed needles. Now, form a triangle of the three needles with the working yarn at the top right of the triangle. Do **not** twist the cast on ridge. With the fourth needle, work across the stitches on the first needle **(Fig. 2)**. You will now have an empty needle with which to knit the stitches from the next needle. Work the first stitch of each needle firmly to prevent gaps. Continue working around without turning the work. If there is a yarn over at the end of the needle, take care **not** to drop it.

Fig. 2

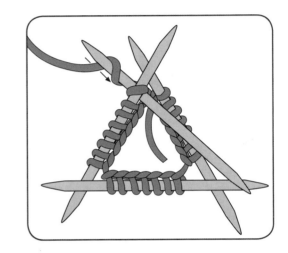

CHANGING COLORS

When changing colors, always pick up the new color yarn from **beneath** the dropped yarn and keep the color which has just been worked to the left of it **(Fig. 3)**. This will prevent holes in the finished piece. Take extra care to keep your tension even.

Fig. 3

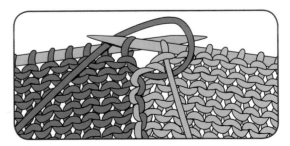

BASIC STITCHES
SLIP KNOT

Make a circle and place the working yarn (the yarn coming from the ball) under the circle *(Fig. 4a)*.

Fig. 4a

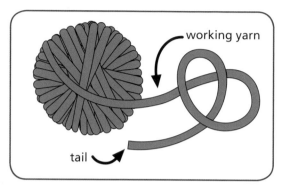

Insert the needle under the bar just made *(Fig. 4b)* and pull on both ends of the yarn to complete the slip knot *(Fig. 4c)*. The slip knot counts as your first cast on stitch.

Fig. 4b

Fig. 4c

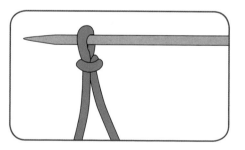

KNIT CAST ON AND ADDING ON STITCHES

The knit cast on is similar to making a knit stitch and placing it on your left needle. This method is also used when you need to add on stitches as in the stair-step triangular shawl designs.

Begin with a slip knot on the needle and hold it in your left hand.

With the working yarn in **back** of the needles, insert the needle held in your right hand into the stitch closest to the tip of the left needle from **left** to **right** *(Fig. 5a)*.

Hold the right needle with your left thumb and index finger while you bring the yarn beneath the right needle and between the needles from **back** to **front** *(Fig. 5b)*.

Fig. 5a   **Fig. 5b**

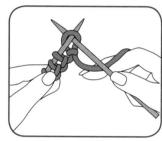   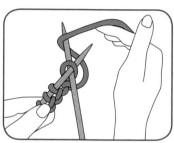

With your right hand, bring the right needle (with the loop of yarn) toward you and back through the stitch *(Figs. 5c & d)*.

Fig. 5c   **Fig. 5d**

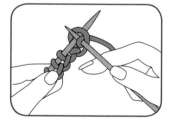   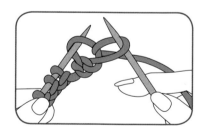

Insert your left needle into the loop just worked from **right** to **left** *(Fig. 5e)* and slip it onto the left needle, gently pulling the working yarn to tighten the new stitch. Repeat for the required number of stitches.

Fig. 5e

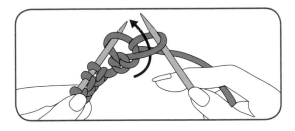

KNIT STITCH *(abbreviated K)*

Hold the needle with the stitches in your left hand. With the working yarn in **back** of the needles, insert the right needle into the stitch closest to the tip of the left needle from **left** to **right** *(Fig. 5a)*.

Hold the right needle with your left thumb and index finger while you bring the yarn beneath the right needle and between the needles from **back** to **front** *(Fig. 5b)*.

With your right hand, bring the right needle (with the loop of yarn) toward you and back through the stitch *(Figs. 5c & d)*, slipping the old stitch off the left needle and gently pulling to tighten the new stitch on the shaft of the right needle.

PURL STITCH *(abbreviated P)*

Hold the needle with the stitches in your left hand. With the working yarn in **front** of the needles, insert the right needle into the stitch closest to the tip of the left needle from **right** to **left** *(Fig. 6a)*.

Hold the right needle with your left thumb and index finger while you bring the yarn **between** the needles from **right** to **left** and around the right needle *(Fig. 6b)*.

Fig. 6a   **Fig. 6b**

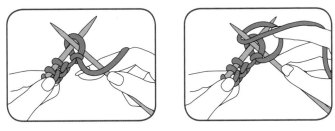

Move the right needle (with the loop of yarn) back through the stitch and away from you *(Fig. 4c)*, slipping the old stitch off the left needle and gently pulling to tighten the new stitch on the shaft of the right needle.

Fig. 6c

INCREASES
MAKE ONE (abbreviated M1)

Insert the **left** needle under the horizontal strand between the stitches from the **front** (*Fig. 7a*); then knit into the **back** of the strand (*Fig. 7b*).

Fig. 7a

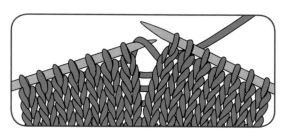

Fig. 7b

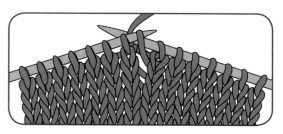

YARN OVERS (abbreviated YO)

A Yarn Over is simply placing the yarn over the right needle creating an extra stitch. Since the Yarn Over does produce a hole in the knit fabric, it is used for a lacy effect. On the row following a Yarn Over, you must be careful to keep it on the needle and treat it as a stitch by knitting or purling it as instructed.

To make a yarn over, you'll loop the yarn over the needle like you would to knit or purl a stitch, bringing it either to the front or the back of the piece so that it'll be ready to work the next stitch, creating a new stitch on the needle as follows:

Between knit stitches

Bring the yarn forward **between** the needles, then back **over** the top of the right hand needle, so that it is now in position to knit the next stitch (*Fig. 8a*).

Fig. 8a

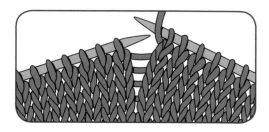

Between purl stitches

Take the yarn **over** the right hand needle to the back, then forward **between** the needles again, so that it is now in position to purl the next stitch (*Fig. 8b*).

Fig. 8b

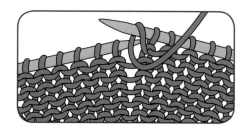

After a knit stitch, before a purl stitch

Bring the yarn forward **between** the needles, then back **over** the top of the right hand needle and forward **between** the needles again, so that it is now in position to purl the next stitch (*Fig. 8c*).

Fig. 8c

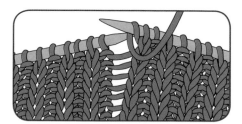

DECREASES
KNIT 2 TOGETHER (abbreviated K2 tog)
Insert the right needle into the **front** of the first two stitches on the left needle as if to **knit** (*Fig. 9*), then **knit** them together as if they were one stitch.

Fig. 9

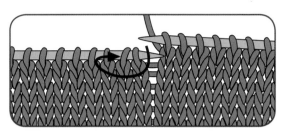

KNIT 2 TOGETHER THROUGH BACK LOOP
Insert the right needle into the **back** of the first two stitches on the left needle as if to **knit** (*Fig. 10*), then **knit** them together as if they were one stitch.

Fig. 10

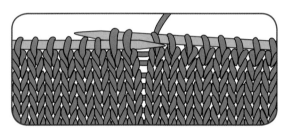

KNIT 3 TOGETHER (abbreviated K3 tog)
Insert the right needle into the **front** of the first three stitches on the left needle as if to **knit** (*Fig. 11*), then **knit** them together as if they were one stitch.

Fig. 11

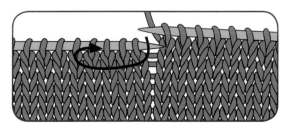

SLIP 1, KNIT 1, PASS SLIPPED STITCH OVER (abbreviated slip 1, K1, PSSO)
Slip one stitch as if to **knit** (*Fig. 12a*). Knit the next stitch. With the left needle, bring the slipped stitch over the knit stitch (*Fig. 12b*) and off the needle.

Fig. 12a

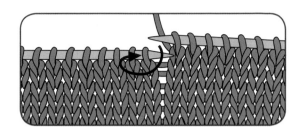

Fig. 12b

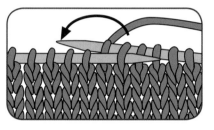

SLIP 1, KNIT 2 TOGETHER, PASS SLIPPED STITCH OVER
(abbreviated slip 1, K2 tog, PSSO)
Slip one stitch as if to **knit** (*Fig. 12a*), then knit the next two stitches together (*Fig. 9*). With the left needle, bring the slipped stitch over the stitch just made (*Fig. 13*) and off the needle.

Fig. 13

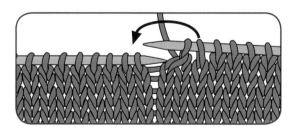

SLIP, SLIP, KNIT (abbreviated SSK)

With yarn in back of the work, separately slip two stitches as if to **knit** *(Fig. 14a)*. Insert the left needle into the **front** of both slipped stitches *(Fig. 14b)* and knit them together as if they were one stitch *(Fig. 14c)*.

Fig. 14a

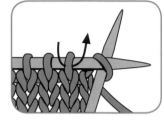

Fig. 14b

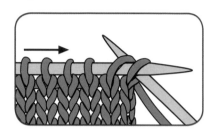

Fig. 14c

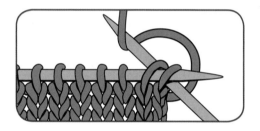

PURL 2 TOGETHER (abbreviated P2 tog)

Insert the right needle into the **front** of the first two stitches on the left needle as if to **purl** *(Fig. 15)*, then **purl** them together as if they were one stitch.

Fig. 15

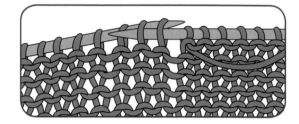

PURL 3 TOGETHER (abbreviated P3 tog)

Insert the right needle into the **front** of the first three stitches on the left needle as if to **purl** *(Fig. 16)*, then **purl** them together as if they were one stitch.

Fig. 16

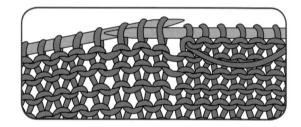

FINISHING
PICKING UP STITCHES

When instructed to pick up stitches, insert the needle from the **front** to the **back** under two strands at the edge of the worked piece *(Fig. 17)*. Put the yarn around the needle as if to **knit**, then bring the needle with the yarn back through the stitch to the right side, resulting in a stitch on the needle.
Repeat this along the edge, picking up the required number of stitches.
A crochet hook may be helpful to pull yarn through.
When instructed to **pick up and knit stitches**, pick up a stitch and slip it onto the left needle, then knit the stitch. Continue for each stitch to be picked up.

Fig. 17

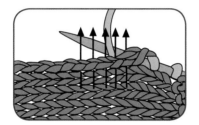

BLOCKING

Blocking helps to smooth your work and give it a professional appearance. Check the yarn label for any special instructions about blocking.

With acrylics that can be blocked, you simply pin your Shawl to the correct size (with rust-proof pins) and cover it with dampened bath towels. When the towels are dry, the garment is blocked.

If the yarn is hand washable, carefully launder your Shawl using a mild soap or detergent, being careful to gently squeeze suds through the piece. Rinse it several times in cool, clear water without wringing or twisting. Remove any excess moisture by rolling it in a succession of dry terry towels. You can put it in the final spin cycle of your washer, without water. Lay the Shawl on a large towel on a flat surface out of direct sunlight. Gently smooth and pat it to the desired size and shape. When it is completely dry, it is blocked.

Another method of blocking, that is especially good for wool, requires a steam iron or a hand-held steamer. Place the Shawl on a flat surface and pin it to the desired size. Hold the steam iron or steamer just above the Shawl and steam it thoroughly. Never let the weight of the iron touch your Shawl because it will flatten the stitches. Never steam ribbings, cables, or intricate raised patterns. Leave the Shawl pinned until it is completely dry.

You can use flexible blocking wires that are stainless steel and rustproof to block your Shawl. Simply insert the wire along the edge of your Shawl and pin the Shawl as needed to your blocking board.

Yarn information

The Shawls in this leaflet were made using a variety of yarns. Any brand of yarn in the specified weight may be used. It is best to refer to the yardage/meters when determining how many balls or skeins to purchase. Remember, to arrive at the finished size, it is the GAUGE/TENSION that is important, not the brand of yarn. For your convenience, listed below are the specific yarns used to create our photography models.

FOR ALL REASONS
Moda Dea® Metro™
#9920 Berry

A HUG TO KEEP
Patons® Nuance
#71130 Nightlife

BECAUSE I CARE
Patons® Shetland Chunky
#03209 Soft Teal

SO NICE TO HAVE YOU AROUND
Bernat® Cool Crochet
#74009 Neopolitan Shades

A LITTLE SOMETHING FOR YOU
TLC® Cotton Plus™
#3100 Cream

THINKING OF YOU
Elsebeth Lavold Designer's Choice Silky Wool
#27 Periwinkle

GIFTS TO SHARE
Moda Dea® Bamboo Wool™
Green - #3650 Bamboo
Lt Green - #3620 Celery

A WISP OF WARMTH
Knit Picks® Alpaca Cloud
#23499 Peppermint Heather

A GIRL'S BEST FRIEND
Red Heart® Soft Yarn™
#1882 Toast

ALWAYS WITH YOU
Lion Brand® Vanna's Choice
Rose - #140 Dusty Rose
Purple - #146 Dusty Purple
Patons® Decor
Brown - #01632 Rich Taupe

For digital downloads of Leisure Art's best-selling designs, visit http://leisureartslibrary.com

We have made every effort to ensure that these instructions are accurate and complete. We cannot, however, be responsible for human error, typographical mistakes, or variations in individual work.

Production Team: Technical Editor - Cathy Hardy; Editorial Writer - Susan McManus Johnson; Artist - Amy Temple; Senior Graphic Artist - Lora Puls; Photo Stylist - Cassie Francioni; Photographer - Jason Masters; Controller - Laura Ogle; and Information Technology Director - Hermine Linz.

Instructions tested and photo models made by JoAnn Bowling, Susan Ackerman Carter, Lee Ellis, Sue Galucki, and Dale Potter.

ISBN 13: 978-1-60140-742-9
ISBN 10: 1-60140-742-4